I0422017

INTJ: 33 Secrets From The Life of an INTJ

Diana Jackson

Contents

1. Enjoys time alone

Positive: Taking the time to recharge one's batteries is something that everyone needs, whether they realize it or not. Luckily, INTJs are introverts who are fully aware of their need for solitude, and they aren't afraid to withdraw before they reach the end of their rope socially. This allows them to avoid getting too exasperated with others (whom they tend to deem incompetent) and keeps them from making those snapping, biting comments to which they can be prone.

Negative: As it happens, INTJs tend to be busy, important people (by virtue of their hard work and ambition), so not being able to get ahold of them or to lure them out of isolation can be a real issue when there are work or family needs that require attending to. INTJs suffer from "always right" syndrome, and feel their alone time is completely justified for as long as they desire, to the consternation of others.

In Relationships: Taking relationships to the "next level" can be tricky, if only because INTJs are picky and refuse to settle. But then there's their penchant for withdrawing, emotionally and physically, which can alienate potential mates who want to, say, move in together. INTJs must simply know that no matter what stage their relationship is in – dating, engaged or married with kids – they have a refuge for when they need to retire and recharge their batteries.

At Work: Their need for time alone informs many INTJs' career choices, so it's not surprising to see them working in positions which give them plenty of independence: a freelance job that allows them to work from home or an office position where they can shut out others' voices and focus on what needs to be done without interruption. INTJs do their best work when they are left to their own devices, because they have the space and time to think thoroughly.

2. Rarely Showers with Praise

Positive: When someone gets a compliment from an INTJ, they know they deserved it. Whether it's a nice painting or a joke, if an INTJ doles out praise – even just one comment – friends and family (and anyone else) can feel as though they have truly done something right, because their personality types are notoriously stingy when it comes to showing appreciation for anything. Consider them the watch-dogs against a society which gives every kid a trophy just for playing.

Negative: On the downside, what is up with those grumps? People around them can feel as though there is never any pleasing them, and then to top it all off, not only are INTJ's prone to a lack of compliments, they may even criticize and attempt to show people the "right" way of doing something (a.k.a "how they would do it"). It can make them unpleasant and grating people to be around, and to make matters worse, they rarely care.

In Relationships: Mates of the INTJ are going to have to have to start looking for the subtle signs of appreciation, because it's not going to come out of their mouths with any great effusion. For sure, partners who stick it out for the long haul will learn to take the distracted thumbs up as their vote of approval, and they will be happy with it. But if INTJs were to go

3

on and on about someone, it would be their mate, provided they chose a complementary match.

At Work: The INTJ in a leadership position can be a fearsome thing, because they hold their standards impossibly high and have no problem expressing their dismay when those lofty goals are not met. Yet employees and even coworkers can learn to work with INTJs if they keep their heads down and their hands/minds busy and continuously strive for the best. A word of positivity from an INTJ can mean the world when it finally comes.

3. Values Work Over Relationships

Positive: Succeeding in the workplace is incredibly important to INTJs – it's why they are among the top two high-earning personality types. In a world where the economy is still stabilizing and unexpected expenses can pop out of nowhere and ruin lives, being a hard worker is a boon, especially since INTJs are known savers who plan ahead with their money. INTJs are also often working in fields where they are improving lives, and their dedication has been known to change the world.

Negative: The negatives to valuing work over relationships are obvious: while INTJs value their solitude and draw energy from it, humans are social creatures who need interaction. The INTJ who lets his relationships suffer because he has gone utterly down the rabbit hole in terms of work can end up on top of the world, but without a friend or partner to share it with. INTJs must take care to be self-aware and to find a balance between work and their loved ones.

In Relationships: The spouse or significant others of an INTJ can find him or herself quite neglected at times, especially in established relationships where feelings have been formalized and the INTJ isn't set to what small "impress" mode they may have been on during courtship. It is important that INTJs make the right match – namely that they choose partners who are strong enough to stand up to them and demand their attention and consideration.

At Work: Employers will likely be thrilled to have someone so hard-working and relentless on their team, and will be happy to let them climb the company hierarchy. Valuing work over relationships may be a phase before settling down, or it could last their entire lives, but INTJs are simply driven by a belief in their own superiority and their ability to do things better than anyone else. At least the rest of the world benefits, since they're usually in science and technology fields.

4. Prefers Intellectual Occupations to Everyday Tasks

Positive: INTJs are game changers and world shakers. As mentioned, they often appear in the sciences and technology, but they can also be able lawyers and businesspeople. At home, their hobbies tend to veer toward the intellectual as well, whether it's reading great works of literature or tinkering in their garage with cars or computers. Through their frequent engagement in stimulating thoughts and activities, on the job or in their leisure time, INTJs are natural problem solvers.

Negative: But the problems of a clean apartment or getting the oil changed can escape them, and those everyday tasks are equally as important, in the overall scheme of things. Yes, humankind clearly needs to be weaned off of fossil fuels with new, green technology, but INTJs also have to emerge from the fog of their important life's work to remember to run their dishwasher before it stinks up their entire home.

In Relationships: Lack of dusting or always putting off that promised task of hanging up some pictures can really grate on the INTJ's partner, so it takes a patient soul to enter into a long-term relationship. Yet INTJs must be equally willing to make an effort now and then. If their mate is as bright, keen and no-nonsense as the INTJ requires, that party should have no problem speaking up about everyday tasks that need doing.

At Work: Can an INTJ work in waste management? Sure, but no matter where they start, they'll probably end up running an entire branch of the operation in months flat. INTJs are simply equipped for intellectual tasks. If their minds aren't being stimulated, they're going to react like bored puppies – acting out, mouthing off, chewing up shoes (okay, maybe not the last one). INTJs have to be challenged at work and not relegated to menial tasks.

5. May Seem Aloof

Positive: Aloofness from an INTJ can be a good thing, because this personality has a tendency to be a little...judgmental. While that in itself is not necessarily positive, their aloof manner can ward off certain individuals who might take such unfriendly attitude personally and prevent a great deal more trouble in the form of personal vendettas formed after a particularly cold and uninterested greeting. Sensitive types will hopefully stay away and find more welcoming company to chat with.

Negative: While INTJs often make the bridge between seeming aloof and being aloof, they are at heart good people who deserve to be appreciated for their dry wit and sharp, on-point sarcasm. Yet if no one wants to approach them, no one finds out what clever personalities lie beneath such an indifferent veneer. And as mentioned, INTJs don't always emphasize relationships in their lives, so it can be even more difficult for them to make those imperative human connections.

In Relationships: If it is difficult for INTJs to make friends at a party, it's a real challenge for them to start and develop relationships. They have to learn to appear as open-minded and creative as they actually are or learn to be happy forever alone. New boyfriends or girlfriends will have to rely on chemistry and the intuitive knowledge that there is actually a really cool and giving person lurking to get past the initial feeling of being judged all the time.

At Work: INTJs prefer to work alone anyway, so if they seem aloof to their coworkers' plans to grab lunch and discuss the latest project, it's usually because they are (unless they have given their coworkers a silent seal of approval). Not "belonging" or "fitting in" to an office culture can drive INTJs to positions that allow them to work from home or with an emphasis on independence, but that is where they thrive anyway – unfettered, undisturbed and focused on the work – not whether people like them.

6. Values Privacy

Positive: Facebook has become a cesspool of oversharing, with people posting their every thought and meal and personal problem for the world to see. INTJs hold themselves aloof from this rabble of attention-seekers, preferring to keep their private lives perfectly private. Indeed, no INTJ is going to get fired for posting inflammatory comments to Twitter or unprofessional snapshots to Instagram. And if they want someone to know something they will contact that person directly.

Negative: Privacy is a good thing, but when INTJs cling to it, it can make them notoriously difficult to get to know and then impossible to relate to. This can lead to an incredibly tight social circle, sometimes limited to just one or two other people, and while INTJs don't need a crowd around them by any means, they could end up missing out on a lot of the friendship and fun that make life worth living.

In Relationships: On the plus side, INTJs are straight-forward communicators who can effectively convey their message without mincing words. Unfortunately, in relationships, "I just want some me time," sounds like "I want to take a break." INTJs aren't going to be the types who rush home to tell their significant other everything about the day, nor will be they forthcoming about their past, including previous relationships. This can be frustrating for more open, transparent partners.

At Work: While it can be difficult for the privacy-loving INTJ to get close to other coworkers – indeed, these personality types can find themselves quite isolated in the workplace socially, as they only begrudgingly share personal information and history – INTJs can also be counted on not to spread office gossip, a rarity in close quarters where all kinds of personal and professional backstabbing can run rife. Count on the INTJ to keep his or her head above board – and their mouth shut.

7. Suspicious of Authority

Positive: INTJs are likely too sensible to go all-out conspiracy theorist, but they do have a healthy suspicion toward authority, and it is not without reason. INTJs are informational sponges who soak up information (like important history lessons) and they have a knack for connecting the dots. This can certainly cause them to view people in positions of power with a dose of skepticism. It may sound troublesome, but it is these types of people who create revolutions that change the world.

Negative: In a lot of cases, though, there is not a lot of sinister going on; people are just living their lives and doing their jobs. Sometimes, INTJs will feel appropriately moved to speak out about their suspicions, and this can cost them not only friends, but in extreme cases their freedom, as well. Depending on how fervent their beliefs and how vocal their outcry may be, they could end up in a fair amount of trouble.

In Relationships: INTJs may gravitate toward like-thinking people who share their beliefs or they may end up opening their eyes to the very real exploitation by people in authority toward those beneath them – it does happen every day. Hopefully, though, before the INTJ can get too zealous their partner can strike the right balance between validating their beliefs and calming them down before they do anything stupid – "stupid" being well-planned and coordinated, but ultimately offensive.

At Work: If anyone is going to figure out that the boss is sleeping with his receptionist and they are jointly embezzling money from the company, it will be the INTJ. Naturally suspicious and rather brilliantly curious, INTJs methodically store away information and data to be sorted through and pieced together when they have the chance to sit and think. In day-to-day matters, this suspicion of authority may manifest itself in INTJs just being pains in the butt.

8. Not Into Nightclubs or Dancing

Positive: Hitting up nightclubs can definitely be a good time if that's the sort of thing you're into, but INTJs just aren't interested in music cranked up so loud that they're deaf for the next day and guzzling down $12 martinis to work up the courage to dance all up on an attractive member of their gender preference. No drunken dancing also means no photographic evidence of unbecoming behavior popping up on social media anywhere.

Negative: Sometimes you just have to put your inhibitions aside and have a good time. Sometimes, you need to dress up, wear a nice cologne or perfume, go out with your friends and get a little hazy. Nobody should be forced to do anything they want, but INTJs are really stubborn about stepping outside of their comfort zones, and it can make them a little stodgy and old before their time.

In Relationships: At least the partners of INTJs don't have to worry about getting texts at 2 a.m. from a friend saying, "LOOK WHAT YOUR BOYFRIEND/GIRLFRIEND IS DOING," followed by a photo of them making out with someone else. Actually, their lack of interest in nightclubs or dancing is indicative of a greater dislike for loud, crowded affairs and their preference for quiet, intimate activities with mates or family-friendly outings for INTJs who have kids.

At Work: Employers of INTJs never have to worry about this personality type calling in sick because they are hungover from being out until 4 a.m. with the rest of the staff. This can certainly endear them to their bosses (in ways their know-it-all attitudes and lack of respect for authority don't), as it makes them appear to be committed, focused and hard-working – which they are. Coworkers may resent them for making everyone else look bad, but luckily INTJs don't really care what anyone else thinks.

9. Prone to Analyzing Things

Positive: Without great analyzers we wouldn't have a judicial system that works, infrastructure that allows us to travel from place to place safely, computers that connect us with family internationally – and the list goes on and on. Analysis literally makes the world go 'round, and INTJs are at the fore of those creative, inquisitive minds. Both in their professional and private lives, INTJs can order everything just the way they want.

Negative: Sometimes, though, we need to act with our gut and not our mind. While INTJs are intuitive, they are prone to over-analysis, to the point where they can miss an opportunity because they are too busy weighing the pros and cons of each possible outcome. Life can pass them by as they retreat into their own minds and search for the best possible answer or solution. There is no telling how many opportunities could open for INTJs if they could act with a bit more impulsivity.

In Relationships: Dating an INTJ can be a lot like taking the SATs: there is a right answer for everything that is asked and you will be evaluated based on your results. INTJs are going to analyze their prospective partners top to bottom (usually with an emphasis on their intelligence and common sense) and they are going to evaluate the state of their relationships not on how it makes them feel, but based on how much sense it makes for them to be together.

At Work: Valuing thoughtful and careful analysis might not make for the most romantic partner, but it does make for an extremely capable employee, one who is destined to create and invent great things that ensure continual progress and the constant bettering of technologies and infrastructures. This is why INTJs are most commonly found in the sciences, like biology, physics and mathematics. Their minds are simply wired toward leaping the obstacles which arise in these fields.

10. Not Easily Impressed

Positive: It seems that these days, certain words get thrown around quite a bit. "Hero" is one; "awesome" is another. The word "epic" is applied in situations where it might not be warranted, too. INTJs are naturally fighting against this trend toward over-application of superlatives, because they just aren't easily won over by mediocre efforts. In the INTJ's mind, no one deserve a gold medal just for showing up; respect and adulation must be earned.

Negative: This can come off as incredibly snooty, though, however good the INTJ's intentions. The truth is, they can't say something is great when it's not, but a little white lie now and then – some tact for the sake of social graces – is as necessary as the mathematics which make computer science possible in making our society an advanced one. INTJs need to work on feigning, if not outright delight, interested appreciation in certain social situations.

In Relationships: No one is going to come calling around an INTJ in a flashy car, wining and dining, and then win over this most skeptical of personalities. If there is one thing to be said for this type, they are not impressed with the superficial trappings that attract some, like model-perfect looks or ostentatious wealth. There has to be substance for a relationship to work, and this helps INTJs pick mates who are ultimately good matches.

At Work: INTJs in positions of authority didn't necessarily strive to be on top, but because one else seemed competent enough, they began their ascent. And that is how they find themselves in charge of projects or offices or even entire departments, demanding nothing but the very best from employees. They are tough but they are fair, and anyone who gets a gold star from their INTJ boss knows it's a double-edged sword – well-earned accolades but a bar set high.

11. Does Not Enjoy Spontaneity

Positive: Spontaneous actions can be exciting, but they aren't always sensible, and terrible things can occur because of them. Look at the activities of most teenagers, who are charged with responsibility – like driving and living on their own at the age of 18 – but haven't fully developed the decision-making part of their brain. INTJs may have seemed like the oldest teenagers ever, because they were only moving forward if a plan was in place, and that becomes an even stronger part of their personality as they age.

Negative: On the downside, though, sometimes the best things in life happen because we take chances. Jobs, relationships, travels, new foods – even if INTJs prefer a less spontaneous existence as it's happening, there will likely come a time when they are much older, reflecting on their lives and regretting all the chances they didn't take. Playing it safe is a comfortable habit, but only by pushing ourselves outside of what we know do we grow as humans.

In Relationships: Even if INTJs aren't the sort to suggest a sudden elopement in Las Vegas, that doesn't mean the spark in their relationship is going to die as the years pass by. INTJs are natural planners and devoted mates, so while a sudden trip is off the table, a surprise trip – one that they have been planning in secret for months – is totally on, to the delight and amazement of their partner.

At Work: While INTJs are notoriously capable workers, their propensity for planning the progress of projects and for organizing their schedules far into the future can make it difficult for them to absorb new and sudden work that must also be completed by a specific deadline. While they are, inwardly, surprisingly flexible employees who can roll with the punches and rearrange their plans, that doesn't necessarily mean they like to, and they certainly won't be happy about it.

12. Likes to Observe

Positive: There is a saying about humans having two eyes and two ears versus one mouth – we are supposedly meant to listen and look twice as much as we speak. INTJs embody this principle as faithful observers who only speak when absolutely necessary, and when they do, it is typically with truth and power on their side, because they have taken the time to let all the facts and information wash over them before methodically analyzing it for meanings others might not glean.

Negative: Sometimes the INTJ tendency for observation can put others off. In a classroom, they might be considered too quiet to earn participation points, and at parties, who knows, they might be pegged as the creeper in the corner who isn't talking to anyone but is staring at people in an uncomfortable and judgmental fashion. This behavior can be isolating and lonely, not to mention frustrating and dangerous, especially if they are around more outspoken people with a fraction of their sense.

In Relationships: It can be difficult for the INTJ's mate to get their partner to speak up and say what's on their mind, and disarming when this personality type seems to sit back and watch as their significant other rages on during an argument. It's not that they are trying to be insensitive or trying to be unfeeling; what they are really trying to do is get a handle on the situation so they can start figuring out how to fix it.

At Work: Much like in a classroom, INTJs are the least likely to start off a brainstorming session at a work meeting. It's not that they are shy or lacking in self-confidence (or opinions); they simply like to take in everyone else's contributions first, while simultaneously reconfiguring their own ideas and suggestions to include the best elements already put forth, so that when they do speak up, they can be as efficient and impactful as possible.

13. Can Seem Insensitive

Positive: There is one in every group of friends – that person who has to open his or her mouth and point out the pink suede elephant in the room. INTJs are that person, and hey, look at it this way – do you want to walk around with lipstick on your teeth or your fly down? You need that "insensitive" person to tell you that you are about to make a fool of yourself in public.

Negative: To people who aren't so personally acquainted with the blunt INTJ, this can be a real turn-off – think Elizabeth Bennett meeting Mr. Darcy and hating him for about 250 pages. INTJs, like all thinking types, are more concerned with telling the truth than being tactful, and unfortunately this tendency can be a bit like autism, where they cannot read the social situation and so they speak or act without grace or seeming concern for others.

In Relationships: It takes a tough cookie to get into the INTJ's heart, and an even tougher person to stick around, because if a male INTJ's wife asks, "Does this skirt make me look fat?" – well, she was better off not seeking his opinion. A good match may attempt to rehabilitate this unfortunate tendency and meet with some success, but on the whole, it's one of those traits that must be accepted as part of the greater person.

At Work: Imagine the INTJ's cubicle neighbor bringing in a picture his little girl drew for Daddy. "Isn't it great?" he asks, delighted, hanging it up. "Well," the INTJ is given to reply, "she obviously hasn't mastered free-hand circles yet." And that is just the tip of the iceberg with these sometimes prickly personalities. They are lucky they are usually so good at their jobs, otherwise they might not have any for sheer perceived insensitivity.

14. Not Religious

Positive: Over the course of human history, if you take an objective look at how things played out, it's clear that religion has caused quite a bit of tension, not to mention violence, bigotry and racism. Even today, hate groups thrive under the visage of religion. INTJs tend to reject religion, and in so doing, they naturally reject religiously overzealous behaviors, thousands of years of religion-based misogyny and creation stories that don't quite match up with scientific fact.

Negative: Racism, misogyny and the like are only one side of the coin, though – so much good is done in the name of religion, from charities and soup kitchens to simple acts of goodwill performed every day. Communities are strong thanks to their religious beliefs, beliefs which in these sad, often violent and tragic days, provide the emotional and spiritual support needed to heal. Further, religious individuals far outnumber non-religious, and there is considerable pressure for INTJs to conform.

In Relationships: Non-religiousness can be a point of contention between the INTJ and his or her partner. It is best that these views are discussed early in a relationship, because reaching the point where both wants to have kids but one wants those children raised Christian, while the INTJ would rather not altogether – it can end in quite a lot of heartbreak or years of tension and mixed messages sent to the kids in question.

At Work: Normally, at work, religious beliefs shouldn't matter, and indeed they usually don't. Religious holidays can be enjoyed in a secular fashion (no non-religious INTJ is going to turn down the opportunity to spend more time with the family!), while religious chatter can be avoided or ignored. The INTJ may or may not provide the dissenting opinion when religion is cited in discussions that pop up in the workplace – it depends on how much energy they wish to expend on the matter.

15. Not Impulsive

Positive: How often do you see something you really can't afford, but go ahead and buy it anyway because you really, really want it? A lot of people do this, and sometimes it's not just a new wallet or a pretty necklace – it can be a car, a house, a huge investment that can end up with the impetuous party filing for bankruptcy. Luckily, INTJs are planners who prefer to set goals and then meet them in due time – and not before.

Negative: A road trip to see a favorite band playing in another state – tonight only! – will be shrugged off as impractical by the pragmatic INTJ, who can miss out on a lot of fun because he or she doesn't want to deviate off their chosen path. They may be truly happy just staying in and reading a book on Nicola Tesla, but they'll never know what a great time they missed out on because they weren't willing to do something a little impulsive on a work night.

In Relationships: A lot of times impulsivity is what keeps the spark alive in long-term relationships, but there is much to be said for stability and security (and INTJs are the ones saying it!). In fact, impulsive acts – like those which constitute adultery – can be downright detrimental to partnerships that are meant to last a lifetime. Partners of the INTJ can be grateful for a mate who at least thinks with his or her head and not the blind lust which drives others.

At Work: INTJs are creative, dynamic thinkers, and while this colors their performance at work – making them innovators of the first water and problem-solvers extraordinaire – even sudden bursts of genius get their due consideration before being put into action. There is no expecting the INTJ to come up with an idea and then immediately run with it; they are going to analyze it from all angles first. But this is what makes them so good at their jobs.

16. Not Prone to Anger

Positive: Annoyance, yes. Judgment, occasionally. But anger – nah, not the INJT, who feels a whole rainbow of emotions before he or she reaches outright anger. And this is good, especially combined with their lack of impulsivity. Because don't many of us wish we could undo things we did in anger – making that damning comment to our mother after she drove us up a wall or keying the cheating ex's car (okay, that one felt good).

Negative: Yet some situations in life are true injustices and they deserve the anger that motivates us to speak out or act out loud to put a stop to cruelty or unfairness. For many INTJs – as for many of all of us – it takes a personal experience with injustice to put on the gloves and come out swinging, and that is a shame, when someone like an INTJ has so many gifts that could be put to good use.

In Relationships: Anger can sound the death knell for relationships, but conversely, sometimes INTJ partners wonder at the robotic lack of emotion from their mates. It's not that INTJs don't feel anything – they aren't sociopaths – it's that they conceal much. But again, these emotions are usually annoyance or judgment, not real anger, which is rare and usually fleeting. INTJs are just too sensible and pragmatic to bear a longstanding grudge against someone they love.

At Work: INTJs, for as much as they prize competency, aren't the sort to blow up at some dullard in the workplace. To their thinking, that is highly inefficient, because it not only solves nothing, it gives the other party the pleasure of knowing they got under the INTJ's skin. Think more along the lines of the silent treatment or a series of patronizing eye rolls – coupled with intensified work ethic, as they decide to really prove who the valuable employee is.

17. Good Time Management Skills

Positive: Time management is a skill that nearly everyone struggles with and could improve, from our personal lives to our work lives, but INTJs are just naturally ahead of the pack when it comes to parceling out the minutes in each day for the tasks that require completion. Because they are also ambitious and hard-working, this makes INTJs formidably effective at achieving their dreams and getting what they want, be it a new car or having enough time to read at the end of the day.

Negative: Have you ever tried to take a vacation with someone who wanted to plot out every single step your group took? As in, "At 9 a.m. we'll head out and grab breakfast, so that by 10 a.m. we can be in the Magic Kingdom, and by 9:15 we should be at the first ride..." and so on. What a drag. Sometimes INTJs don't know how to let the day flow. Not every moment has to be assigned a task!

In Relationships: INTJs are funny in relationships, because their approach is so pragmatic. There's no telling where they get the idea that things should progress at a certain rate, but there they are, thinking that if they are still with someone by 10 months, they should think about moving in. Not because they really like each other (which they sincerely do, or else they wouldn't still be around), but because it's the logical next step.

At Work: Here is where INTJs really shine in the workplace. Actually, their ability to manage time is likely what got them to such a good job in the first place – being able to pace their schoolwork in college so that they are always well-prepared for tests and never rushed on essays. In their professional lives they are just the same and even better after years of practice, making them reliable, responsible and worthy of promotions and accolades.

18. Doesn't Care for Prestige or Symbols of Wealth

Positive: Some of the most atrocious people out there are the ones who flaunt their wealth. It's all well and good to have money and to spend money on nice things, but it gets obnoxious when a person is a walking billboard for labels and can only make conversation about the latest designer bag or sports car. INTJs tend to be high earners, but you'd never know it based on how they act – which is with a great deal of material humility.

Negative: This can make them seem a bit stingy, especially since they do tend to buy what they want, when they want it, but may insist that others, including their family members and especially their kids, wait or not get the item at all. Further, prestige isn't always a bad thing, especially when it's a brilliant invention. If the INTJ doesn't step up to claim the idea, they can be assured that someone else will gladly take the credit.

In Relationships: People who shun ostentatious shows of wealth are going to be more likely to find partners who care about them for who they really are, not what they can buy. This works in the INTJ's favor, as it helps weed out clingers-on who would otherwise see dollar signs. Instead, they will be in a good way to find sincere and genuine significant others whom they can privately spoil or surprise.

At Work: No INTJ is going to make enemies in the workplace on account of his or her boisterous boastfulness. This just isn't the personality type to make a big deal out of a raise or a promotion – they are more likely to wear a small smile in secret, privately pleased. While he or she certainly feels it is warranted, this type is too practical to flaunt the outward trappings of success in a way that would disrupt their relations with coworkers.

19. Not Suggestible

Positive: There's the INTJ way of doing something and then there's the wrong way. Those are the only two options, and while it can be loathsome for people around the INTJ to always have to compromise, there is no denying that with their combination of intelligence, resourcefulness and knack for penetrating analysis makes this personality type thoroughly capable problem solvers who not only have an answer for pretty much everything, they have a great answer.

Negative: But no one is perfect, and even INTJs can be blinded by their own perceived brilliance. Thus, it's easy for them to make an obvious mistake – obvious to everyone else around them – that causes everyone else loss of time or resources. And their stubbornness is legendary, making every argument an utter trial because INTJs simply do not feel that they need anyone else's input. As far as they are misguidedly concerned, they can do everything better alone.

In Relationships: Anyone who has dated a know-it-all can attest that it gets really, really annoying. What INTJs need is a personality with the same self-assurance and confidence, but with a twist of cleverness to manipulate them into learning how to compromise and take suggestion from others. It must be done with subtlety and guile, which are good matches for the INTJ's self-righteousness. INTJs who have found this paragon of a partner won't even realize the extent to which they are being bettered.

At Work: Most work places require some kind of team work, and someone inevitably has to take the lead and give the group focus. This will likely end up being the INTJ in the room, not because he or she particularly relishes leadership, but because in their view, no one else is competent enough or has good enough ideas and vision. Coworkers might get annoyed at having their ideas steamrolled, so INTJs should work on at least feigning interest in what others have to say.

20. Distrusts Emotions

Positive: Emotions – who needs them? Look at Peter Abelard, a medieval scholar who was the rising star of Paris society. He fell in love with his landlord's niece and ended up castrated and shut up in a monastery. So not every situation involving emotions is going to end up like poor Abelard's, but you can bet that level-headed thinking, as much removed from emotional influence as possible, is the INTJ trademark for decision-making and it has spared them tons of bad decisions.

Negative: Without emotions, though, the most beautiful things in the world would not exist. There would be no poetry, no paintings, no music. These are the products of love, hate, anger and joy, and while their makers often lived tumultuous, unpredictable lives, they felt with an astonishing fullness. If INTJs ruled the world, we might have the technology for individual hovercrafts, but there would be no Sistine Chapel ceiling or Canon in D or movies.

In Relationships: At some point, INTJs are going to have to reach out and try to develop a feeling aspect, because no one wants to date a robot who makes all their relationship decisions based on sense and reason. Luckily, there are tons of feeling, nurturing, patient individuals out there who can act as a counter-balance to their INTJ's stolid logistical bent. Often,

INTJs distrust emotions because they got hurt once; they must learn that it's just another part of living.

At Work: This distrust of emotion is part of what drives INTJs into the fields they tend to choose – sciences, math, legal professions and business. Emphasis is instead placed on reason and logic, on justice meted out based on merit, rather than emotional reactions like anger and vengeance. INTJs fill careers in these fields admirably, and while they aren't necessarily serving the public the way counselors and social workers do, their impact on and improvement of society is enormous.

21. Neat and Organized in Personal Habits

Positive: A home that is ready for guests at a moment's notice is no small thing, nor a car that looks as though it saw a vacuum cleaner just the other day. The INTJ is especially meticulous when it comes to his or her personal space, which is really an inviting and pleasant part of their character (a nice way to off-set their rather critical persona). A clean, uncluttered personal life also indicates that they take good care of their belongings – considering how hard they work to attain them.

Negative: INTJs who go too far down the rabbit hole can get a little OCD, though, insisting that this spatula goes in this drawer but this other spatula, because it is older and also a different color, should go in another drawer. Does their organization make sense to anyone but themselves? Maybe not, and it can definitely come off a little eccentric (if endearing). Roommates, too, may have a heck of a time adjusting to the demanding cleanliness standards set by an INTJ.

In Relationships: What sets significant others apart from roommates is that significant others can and will usually have the comfort level and security to speak up and tell their INTJ mate that they are going overboard. But at the same time, who is going to argue if the other person in the house enjoys that feeling of accomplishment when the kitchen is sparkly clean before going to bed? Clutter, too, is a common misfortune for settled couples, but INTJs will methodically assign items to a sensible spot.

At Work: Those personal habits will likely spill over into their professional lives, but this can only be to the good. Having a neat desk with everything in its correct place ensure that important and sensitive documents – and INTJs tend to have jobs where a misplaced item can stall a project entirely and waste tons of company money – are securely but easily located if they are needed in a jiffy. It's just another facet of their reliability as employees.

22. Socially Awkward

Positive: Not everyone has to be the shining star in a crowd, and INTJs certainly aren't that. They might stutter or say the wrong thing at the wrong time or cringe when they have to hang out in large crowds, but at least they know who they are and how to be honest about that. They can deal accordingly, whether it's withdrawing from company when their introverted selves have run out of steam or simply staying among close-knit groups of friends whom they trust.

Negative: The socially awkward one may blend in occasionally, but the INTJ was born to stand out by virtue of his or her lack of self-censorship. Again, they will be the ones who say the impossibly insensitive things. It's not that they're doing it out of malice or intention to be mean, but their awkwardness in social situations can open the dam that's already weakened by their stalled sensitivity – that is, they blurt out the first thing on their mind.

In Relationships: It can be difficult for the significant others of INTJs to integrate them into their social lives, since this personality type would much rather skip the family dinner or work function and stay home to write the computer program they've been working on. And then there are events that cannot be avoided, and so it is best if the INTJ's partner preps their company – be it family, friends or coworkers – well in advance.

At Work: INTJs are probably less likely to care if they are considered socially awkward at work, because they are there to work – not find new best friends. Sometimes, though, they'll avoid the whole matter of not fitting in by working in solitary professions where there isn't a lot of chit-chat or small talk necessary to get through the day. This is where freelance journalism or even attorney services can be the go-to professions for INTJs who still have a lot to offer.

23. Quiet in Large Groups

Positive: Again, not everyone needs to be the loud mouth that dominates the conversation. In fact, INTJs probably detest that person that everyone knows is just talking because they like the sound of their own voice. INTJs might not be the most active participants in lively conversations or parties, but that doesn't mean they have checked out. They are broadly observant and can be counted up on to recall minute details that could come in handy later.

Negative: Not everyone responds well to the one person in the group who isn't saying much and just seems to be hanging around without invitation or contribution. It isn't that being quiet in large groups itself is a negative, but rather that how it can be construed by others can be damning, especially if those others are the suspicious sort. INTJs may find their loyalties tested again and again because they choose not to be so brazen about their beliefs.

In Relationships: Luckily, relationships tend to be just two people, and the significant other of an INTJ can get their mate to open up with the proper prodding. More social situations can be a problem, especially in family gatherings with a large, boisterous crowd, and while the INTJ might not have much to contribute to the joking and teasing, you can bet they are the ones who notice that Aunt Sally was hiding pain behind her eyes – and then it comes out she is getting divorced from Uncle Randy.

At Work: The INTJ is usually pretty consistent in personality traits, so the same quietness that they display at work in groups was probably the norm in college and even high school. They just don't feel the need to speak up – until they really do. Their MO is to let the conversation flow but only say something when – after careful observation and analysis of the situation – they feel they can offer something truly helpful to the discussion.

24. Dislikes Crowds

Positive: Crowds can be dangerous. Crowds can cause you to lose sight of what's important. They are sometimes jostling, sometimes stressful to maneuver. You won't catch the INTJ out Christmas shopping in the weeks leading up to the big day, because he or she is having none of that annoying, rude crap. INTJs stay above the fray and find clever ways to avoid mass groups of people – like shopping online or streaming a live concert on their laptop or even finding ways to streamline the airport experience.

Negative: Sometimes, though, you cannot avoid getting caught up in a big mass of bodies, and INTJs – who aren't shy about voicing their dislike – can make that incredibly uncomfortable, to say nothing about unpleasant. If they're the type who will be short with a salesclerk or a waiter because the crowded spot caused them to wait and get pushed around a bit or bumped into, INTJs can make life miserable for everyone in the vicinity.

In Relationships: Well, the individuals dating their beloved INTJ might have a tough time getting this personality type out to bars or shows unless they know it won't be too busy. In fact, a lot of shared activities may end up being restructured or rescheduled around when it should be the least active with other people. And hey, that's not a wholly bad thing – if you can swing grocery shopping at 11 p.m., why not?

At Work: Dislike of crowds often influences the INTJ from taking jobs that require too much social interaction in large groups of people – even when they're younger, like in college, and might be limited in available options. INTJs are hard workers but they are also smart workers, and they seek out positions that, even if they exist among a large number of coworkers, at least affords them independence and autonomy at their desk.

25. Prefers a Seat in the Aisle or Next to the Exit

Positive: There is nothing wrong with not wanting to be closed into a seating arrangement where you could end up having to go pee but then disrupt half the row as you attempt to make a graceful exit. INTJs know this and they tend to nab that last seat, closest to the aisle and near to an exit, whether it's planes or theaters or even restaurant booths. It is one of the ways INTJs show their consideration for others, as well as a shrewd move.

Negative: If they are stuck all the way at the end of a row, however, with no one else around them, it can make INTJs look a little unapproachable and even unfriendly, as if they are unwilling to mix with the rest of the crowd. On planes, insisting that they sit near the aisle also means that they're going to miss the view out of the window – a view which, let's face it, helps to put our own place in this world into some kind of perspective.

In Relationships: As long as the INTJ doesn't match up with a like-minded individual on this particular issue, all will be well. In fact, their partner might come to appreciate the logic behind having a quick point of exit after a long instrumental concert or the ability to get up to use the restroom and only disrupt one person's view during a movie (the INTJ's, of course, who can lift his or her knees to easily accommodate them).

At Work: Since INTJs are probably going to think fluffy fundraisers and seminars are a waste of their time (provided none of their own personal heroes are present as keynote speakers), their wanting an end seat has every likelihood of enabling an early retreat or a hasty exit after what they perceive to be a boring presentation. INTJs will be INTJs and there's just nothing to be done about that.

26. Strives for Efficiency

Positive: One of the most obvious defining traits of any INTJ is his or her desire to live the most efficient life possible. This means not wasting time or resources, and it springs from their thinking and judgment aspects, where logic, analysis and organization work as one to create a doing machine who bends the world to his or her will. For sure, when you are efficient, you get things done, whether it's cleaning the house or churning out work projects ahead of schedule.

Negative: Yet someone who is always trying to be efficient can forget about that other part of life where you need to just chill and live and breathe. Humans aren't on this planet to be robots in some vast assembly line factory; we're here to experience things and be spontaneous and yes, even make mistakes. Sometimes, though, mistakes are what set us on a course toward even better results, and INTJs can miss those opportunities.

In Relationships: It might seem strange operating within a relationship to maximize "happiness" or "contentment," but that is often what INTJs can do if they are not pulled out of their own heads and made to stop and smell the roses. Left to their own devices, it makes sense to an INTJ that they should do this or that action based on how it will make the relationship more harmonious – not based on how it makes either party feel.

At Work: In the office or on the job, however, this attainment of efficiency marks the INTJ out as a star employee and one to watch. It makes them formidable as a person of authority – underlings will constantly wonder how their manager gets so much done in so little time – and it challenges and inspires others to reach their level of efficiency. It can make the INTJ the subject of some resentment, though, as others struggle to keep up.

27. Wants People to Make Sense

Positive: Their thinking aspect plays into their personality to a huge extent, and it informs their love of logic. Not just science and math, mind you, but how they interact with others and want for others to interact with them. And if they might stop someone mid-argument and ask them to clarify a point or go into further detail, they aren't being patronizing – they genuinely want to be able to follow a point's logic so that they can try to understand where the other person is coming from.

Negative: As scary as it can be, sometimes people do things that make absolutely zero sense. They do crazy things for no reason, and maybe it's a chemical imbalance or some long-suppressed feeling that came bubbling up, but either way, it cannot be explained. This is vexing to the INTJ, who will either doggedly pursue the truth, only to wind up themselves in a bit of a crazed state or write that person off entirely as not worth associating with.

In Relationships: Relationships seem to be the arena where feelings most often take over and logic gets pushed to one side. Individuals within a couple can have irrational responses that spontaneous and emotions-based, and if an INTJ is matched with someone like that, it can make the partnership a very damaging and toxic one. INTJs may come to care deeply for someone, but if there is a disconnect with communication, it just won't work.

At Work: INTJs can be prickly to work with; if they are fixing you with a steely glare then they are clearly indicating that think you are part of the problem. The best way to avoid this fate is to base your words and deeds on sound logic. Sure, INTJs could be more accepting and less judgmental of others, but that probably won't happen. The workplace is the INTJ's world, and the rest of us just get to hang out there.

28. Has Trouble Talking About Feelings

Positive: It is interesting when a personality type has a difficult time talking about their feelings, because INTJs fall into that category – yet they experience the full range of emotions like anyone else. Their difficulty discussing anger or frustration can be a plus, though, because they will avoid saying something that cannot be taken back, and then in the meantime, probably figure out a way to solve the problem meaningfully.

Negative: A person can only stay dammed up for so long, however, and if the INTJ suppresses their emotions for too long, they can end up going ballistic in an epic and spectacular fashion, possibly on someone who happened to look at them wrong. Not expression their feelings can also lead to higher levels of stress, which is linked with high blood pressure and bad sleep habits, to say nothing of bad relations with friends, family and coworkers.

In Relationships: A more feeling personality type might look at the INTJ and see something akin to the innards of a hard drive: discs and pieces and lights whirring and blinking, indicating life, but no emotions. INTJs can either find like-minded mates or - perhaps more to their benefit – attach to someone who lives life with passion and spontaneity and encourages them to open up more often about how they're feeling (so long as they can do so with a deft touch).

At Work: Part of the reason INTJs can be difficult to work with is because they don't really open up to their coworkers – certainly not about things that are going on at home, and rarely about how events in the workplace are making them feel. This closed-off barrier-type approach to existing in an office or other setting makes it difficult to resolve lingering tensions, so it helps if INTJs can try to meet their coworkers somewhere in the middle.

29. Systematic and Analytical

Positive: Systematic and analytical ways of thinking are what give INTJs their efficiency and ability to be so productive. These types aren't going to win any Pulitzers for imaginative fiction, but they are going to be the ones who started young by winning the science fair and then went on to receive prestigious fellowships and grant funding. They don't get easily overwhelmed because their minds have the ability to break a problem down step by step and figure out the best plan of attack.

Negative: Sometimes a problem just isn't a matter for systematics and analytics – it's about what is inside one's heart, and you have to act fast, on impulse, if you don't want to lose something or someone dear to you. INTJs don't stop and smell the roses – they stop and classify them, they stop to put the petals under a microscope and vivisect the stems to learn how the rose works and why it smells the way it does.

In Relationships: The flavor of an INTJ's relationship might feel a little bland to others, and maybe even to their partner if that person is of a more feeling aspect, but their tendency to analyze situations for efficiency and pragmatics does create true stability. They are providers, too, often with well-paying jobs, and while they might not speak love, they feel it and want to share their lives with one special person whom they love.

At Work: No matter what job INTJs might hold throughout their lives, from when they started at a fast food joint (where they quickly figured out the most methodical and efficient way to get through a dinner rush) to their ascent to lead surgeon at a renowned hospital, they are taking in information and data and puzzling out how best to do their job – and how best everyone could be doing theirs, too.

30. Sometimes Has a Hidden Romantic Side

Positive: Yes, even the INTJ, under all that cool reserve and patronizing condescension, even this personality type has a romantic and tender core. It's just a matter of tapping it, because it can be as elusive as sweet spring water in a forest. While that might not sound promising to many people, to those who appreciate the INTJ for his or her mechanic brilliance this extra, hidden layer is quite a pleasant and delightful surprise.

Negative: But INTJs, who don't like to appear weak and who refuse to make decisions based on what their heart says, can bury that romantic side pretty deep, to the point that it can take people years to really find it. Further, INTJs might be embarrassed by their desire for passion and their longing for a little poetry or piano music, and may make a concentrated attempt to conceal it from the world – working against their very nature and leading to great emotional conflict that they can't express.

In Relationships: One thing is for sure: the partner who discovers his or her INTJ's romantic side knows just how much they are cherished. The kind of logical thoughtfulness that works in their favor professionally is also a boon personally, as they plot and plan the very best and most touching surprises out there. These are the types who pull off those amazingly complex proposals that end up on YouTube. There's nothing cold or emotionless about that!

At Work: For the INTJ, their romantic side is just something else to conceal from coworkers. They simply don't feel the need to share their private lives with anyone in the professional setting, and this especially can reveal them at their most vulnerable and raw. If anyone is let in on the secret, you can bet that individual is sworn to secrecy upon pain of death – or worse, being held in utter contempt and losing all of the INTJ's trust.

31. Tends to be Skeptical

Positive: Skepticism is a good thing in many situations, like letters asking for a small donation now and promising a huge bank deposit later or even promising cancer research which is hopeful but can't yet stand up to peer review. Skepticism makes the world try harder and do better, and it makes the products we use – like medicine, pet foods, cars and even toasters safer, more reliable. A healthy dose of skepticism, such as the INTJ has, is a lot more practical than a great deal of gullibility.

Negative: Skepticism can be damaging in some situations, though. INTJs tend to lay it on pretty thick, too – if something doesn't seem to make sense to them or doesn't impress them upon first viewing, their reactions can be chilly at best or outright cruel at worst. And then there is the fact that INTJs can inadvertently stall progress by discouraging someone so deeply that they give up, when they were just steps away from a breakthrough.

In Relationships: These days, skepticism is definitely more valuable when dating than open-ended trust. That's a shame, but there are just too many people out there who are willing to take advantage of others for their own game. But street-smart INTJs aren't likely to be taken in by a charming, good-looking fake. They are not only skeptical, they are cynical, and to tell the truth, they are probably expecting someone to come along and try to pull one over them.

At Work: As long as INTJs can temper their skepticism with encouragement and show a little appreciation now and then, they will do all right in the workplace among their fellow coworkers. If not, they might end up ostracized – certainly, no one is going to want to work with them or for them, not when it seems like no matter what you do it's just not good enough for the discerning INTJ.

32. Prone to Holding Back Emotions

Positive: Stoicism is a lost art, but INTJs have it on lock-down. In situations where other people would be losing their minds – and causing a chain reaction of frenzy or panic among others – your INTJ is maintaining a cool, even demeanor that might not be soothing, but at least it doesn't contribute to the chaos. Robotic they might be, but these personality types are going to voice reason and sense before raw human emotion and we're all better off for it in many instances.

Negative: Holding powerful personal feelings in, however, can be a recipe for disaster. INTJs who spend years not letting out their true feelings can suffer physically for emotional woes. Their hair can fall out, they could develop maladies that never fully go away, they can age visibly in less time than their contemporaries...and the list goes on and on, to say nothing of what it does, physically, to their hearts. Unexpressed emotion tends to become chronic stress that frankly stresses out the body until it starts to shut down.

In Relationships: Even if INTJs find other personality types that hold their emotions in, it's like two batteries loaded into a device both facing the same way – the device can't power on because the batteries are incompatible the way they've been placed. Without communication there can be no real relationship, so INTJs would do better to challenge themselves with partners who demand to hear the emotional truth. Practice makes perfect.

At Work: From the bedroom to the boardroom, INTJs suppress a lot of what they are truly feeling because they value emotional decisions less and well-thought out courses of action more. But while that might mean they are holding down a serious outburst of anger and frustration at someone who crossed them at work, they will hint at this deep-down explosion in their gut with truly artistic displays of condescension. There can be no doubt who the INTJ keeps on their "list."

33. Natural Planner and Organizer

Positive: The planning and organizing talent that INTJs possess is all thanks to their judging aspect, which enjoys predictability and values long-term commitments. This makes the INTJ a demonstrably reliable and responsible person to have around and helps them create a good, stable life that is financially secure and comfortable. Inside that home (and on the job) everything has a proper place and if some new item needs to be integrated, they find the best, most logical location for it.

Negative: More perceiving types will likely be horrified by what they would look at as the INTJ's rigidity and unbending nature. They would argue that planning and organization are great – but only to a point. Sometimes we really are better off just letting events and situations unfold as they will – not trying to force things to happen when they aren't meant to be. For a non-religious type, INTJs are awfully keen on playing god.

In Relationships: Even if spontaneity might be absent from relationships, at least when one partner asks, "What should we do for date night?" the INTJ will throw him or herself into a blueprint for a fun evening; think about that the next time you and your significant other go back and forth with "I don't care" when one of you asks where you should get dinner. The planning/organizing trait also means that trips and surprise parties will be meticulously plotted and go off without a hitch. Bravo, INTJ.

At Work: Employers who can take the INTJ superiority complex in stride will be absolutely delighted by their employees' capable willingness to commit to long-term projects and assignments and their ability to pace the work so that it is completed in due time. These people aren't afraid to sink months or even years into their work – which is especially important for scientists who require that much time and tenacity to see research become reality in the form of machines and medicine.

www.ingramcontent.com/pod-product-compliance
Lightning Source LLC
Chambersburg PA
CBHW070812290526
45795CB00002B/689